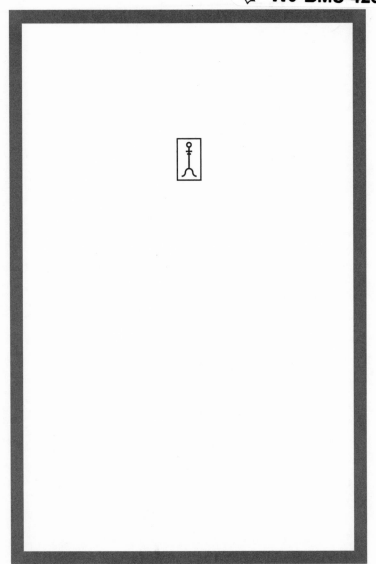

Still MORE GEORGE W Bushisms

Neither in French, nor in English, nor in Mexican

EDITED BY JACOB WEISBERG

with a Foreword by Al Franken

A FIRESIDE BOOK

Published by Simon & Schuster

New York London Toronto Sydney Singapore

Fireside
Rockefeller Center
1230 Avenue of the Americas
New York, NY 10020

Copyright © 2003 by Jacob Weisberg
Foreword copyright © 2003 by Al Franken

FIRESIDE and colophon are registered trademarks of Simon & Schuster, Inc.

For information regarding special discounts for bulk purchases, please contact Simon
& Schuster Special Sales at 1-800-456-6798 or business@simonandschuster.com

Designed by Joy O'Meara Battista

Manufactured in the United States of America

1 3 5 7 9 10 8 6 4 2

Library of Congress Cataloging-in-Publication Data
Bush, George W. (George Walker), 1946–
Still more George W. Bushisms : neither in French, nor in English, nor in Mexican /
edited by Jacob Weisberg ; with a foreword by Al Franken.
p. cm.
"A Fireside book."
1. Bush, George W. (George Walker), 1946– —Humor. 2. Bush, George W.
(George Walker), 1946– —Quotations. 3. Bush, George W. (George Walker), 1946–
—Language. 4. Malapropisms. 5. United States—Politics and government—
2001—Humor. 6. United States—Politics and government—2001—
Quotations, maxims, etc. I. Title.
E903.3 .B88   2003   352.23'8'0973—dc22   2003061695
ISBN 0-7432-5100-8

FOREWORD BY AL FRANKEN

Along with a whole pack of other journalists, Jacob Weisberg covered Governor George W. Bush during the long months of the 2000 presidential campaign. Every single one of those journalists heard Bush make one stupid remark after another, day after day:

"I know how hard it is for you to put food on your family."

"Families is where our nation finds hope, where wings take dream."

"They want the federal government controlling Social Security like it's some kind of federal program."

Yet it was Weisberg alone who understood the commercial potential for collecting these idiotic remarks in the form of a small trade paperback book, the kind that could be kept by the toilet, and picked up now and then for a few moments of distraction and some surefire laughs.

This is the third in the series. Fortunately, for Weisberg, the president continues to have problems either forming ideas in his head or expressing those ideas when he opens his mouth. And so the *Bushisms* series has become quite the gravy train for Weisberg, a dream come true for any political writer, because it actually involves no writing.

In fact, it seems, I am the only one doing any writing for this book at all. And yet, when Weisberg puts together his curriculum vitae, it will include three international bestsellers. Yes, these books are popular not only in the United States—and in places like Germany, France, and Italy, where Bush is considered an out-of-control cowboy—but also in countries that made up the Coalition of the Willing against Iraq. Countries like England, Poland, Tonga, and the Solomon Islands.

And, as an American, that worries me to some extent. It is one thing to have the rest of the world believe that our president cannot be trusted. It is quite another for them to think he is stupid.

Because he is not. It has taken me some time to come to this point of view. You see, facility with language is only one aspect of intelligence. Bush, as I have come to appreciate, is a shrewd, if dishonest, politician who surrounds himself with like-minded advisers.

"Compassionate Conservatism." "By far a vast majority of my tax cuts go to those at the bottom." "No Child Left Behind"—the most ironically named piece of legislation since the 1942 "Japanese Family Leave Act." All these in their way are as funny as any of the malapropisms in this volume.

And there may even be some method to Bush's seeming stupidity. Take, for example, when he told us during the 2000 campaign that he doesn't mind being "misunderestimated." Sure, this sounded crazily dumb. But maybe in his own way he was outsmarting us all. Maybe by "misunderestimated," he meant that he doesn't mind being underestimated *for the wrong reason*. It was okay that we thought he was stupid. Hell, that lowered expectations for the debates. What we were really underestimating was his capacity to fool us.

Take another example. "Subliminable." Remember how during the campaign he said "subliminable" four times after being asked whether a Republican ad had used the word "rats" subliminally? Maybe by saying "subliminable" so many times, Bush was himself using a subtle subliminal technique to give people the unconscious mes-

sage that he was "able" to be president. "Subliminable . . .
subliming-able . . . subliminably I am "able" to be president." Got it?

So, go ahead. Laugh at the dumb things President
Bush has said over the past year or so. But don't be fooled.
He's less stupid than you think.

INTRODUCTION

This year, Bushisms went global. As the ramp up to the Gulf War accelerated through the summer and fall of 2002, our syntactically challenged president did nothing to disguise his disdain for the views of those countries known in his father's day as "the allies." The nations of Europe responded to this insult in kind—by buying my book.

In the United States, this series has attempted to bridge the divide between Bush detractors (who laugh at him) and Bush supporters (who can laugh with him). All remain welcome. But there's no hiding that the recent vogue for Bushisms in ol' Europe is primarily an expression of hostility toward Bush II and Gulf War II. Having been informed just how little their opinions matter inside the White House, members of the European Community comfort themselves with the notion that its current occupant is—let us not mince words—a semiliterate moron.

That is not to say that the world scorns Bush in a uniform manner. Though the feeling that Bush is a fool is common throughout Europe, the cadences vary from country to country. In Great Britain, where Bushisms supply fodder for a seemingly endless number of newspaper columnists, the notion of an American leader who lacks fluency in English is taken as vastly amusing. The British see Bush as a hip-shooting cowboy, but somehow a comic one—Dr. Strangelove, yes, but with some Bart Simpson thrown in. Having survived the Reagan-Thatcher romance, they are not unduly alarmed.

The French, by comparison, seethe. They take *le président américain* for a corporate lackey, an ignorant imperialist, and a Texan religious fanatic. And they blame all of us for hiring him. In this joyless spirit, a well-known French publisher agreed to buy the translation rights to *George W. Bushisms,* then phoned back to say he would not be offering payment after all, as he had found the same material for free on an American website (mine!). I have been filling Evian bottles with tap water ever since and serving it to my guests. So far, no one has noticed any difference.

As for the Germans, they appear alternately amused and horrified. *Voll daneben, Mr. President! (Well Said, Mr. President)* presents itself as both a joke book and a conclusive indictment. During the war, it shared Deutsch bestseller status with Bob Woodward's *Amerika im Krieg (Bush at War)*, which presumably sold to more Rumsfeld-friendly readers. Much as I appreciate the sales, there is something intrinsically hilarious about translating these nuggets—and even more hilarious about rendering them into German. Most read as if unsuccessfully translated from German in the first place. Which really came first: *"Meine Aussenpolitik wird ausgewogen sein"* or "I will have a foreign-handed foreign policy"?

All of these Bushisms are previously uncollected, but in a break with previous practice, not all of them are new—uttered in the past year. While pulling together a 2004 George W. Bushisms Calendar (available near the bookstore table where you are Frenchily reading this without intending to buy), my helper David Newman unearthed some older gems that somehow evaded previous anthologizing.

This ongoing project has given me a paradoxical interest in both Bush bashing (foreign sales!) and Bush's reelection (volumes IV, V, and VI!). I continue to ignore such incentives and simply offer up what I find.

Jacob Weisberg
August 2003

Still
MORE
GEORGE
W
Bushisms

UNEXPECTED

"I'm the master of low expectations."

—Aboard Air Force One, June 4, 2003

LAST RETORT

"Other Republican candidates may retort to personal attacks and negative ads."

—*Fund-raising letter from George W. Bush, quoted in* The Washington Post, *March 24, 2000*

L'ÉTAT, C'EST MOI

"I know something about being a government. And you've got a good one."

—*Stumping for Governor Mike Huckabee, Bentonville, Arkansas, November 4, 2002*

FINANCIER

"I recently met with the finance minister of
the Palestinian Authority, was very
impressed by his grasp of finances."

—*Washington, D.C., May 29, 2003*

POOR BUT PROUD

"First, let me make it very clear, poor people
aren't necessarily killers. Just because you
happen to be not rich doesn't mean you're
willing to kill."

—*Washington, D.C., May 19, 2003*

GETTING READY

"There may be some tough times here in America. But this country has gone through tough times before, and we're going to do it again."

—Waco, Texas, August 13, 2002

DANGER I

"I think war is a dangerous place."

—Washington, D.C., May 7, 2003

DANGER II

"Iran would be dangerous if they have a nuclear weapon."

—Washington, D.C., July 18, 2003

TRUST BUT VERIFY

"I think the American people—I hope the American—I don't think, let me—I hope the American people trust me."

—*Washington, D.C., December 18, 2002*

HOPE

"If a person doesn't have the capacity that we all want that person to have, I suspect hope is in the far distant future, if at all."

—*Washington, D.C., May 22, 2001*

CURRENT AFFAIRS

"I don't remember debates. I don't think we spent a lot of time debating it. Maybe we did, but I don't remember."

—On discussions of the Vietnam War when he was an undergraduate at Yale, The Washington Post, *July 27, 1999*

THE EDUCATION PRESIDENT

"I read the newspaper."

—In answer to a question about his reading habits, New Hampshire Republican debate, December 2, 1999

AMERICAN KNOW-HOW

"I'm thrilled to be here in the breadbasket of America because it gives me a chance to remind our fellow citizens that we have an advantage here in America—we can feed ourselves."

—Stockton, California, August 23, 2002

SHORTCUT

"I can assure you that, even though I won't be sitting through every single moment of the seminars, nor will the vice president, we will look at the summaries."

—*Waco, Texas, August 13, 2002*

SECRETARIES' DAY

"All up and down the different aspects of our society, we had meaningful discussions. Not only in the Cabinet Room, but prior to this and after this day, our secretaries, respective secretaries, will continue to interact to create the conditions necessary for prosperity to reign."

—*Washington, D.C., May 19, 2003*

SECRETARIES II

**"And, most importantly, Alma Powell,
secretary of Colin Powell, is with us."**

—Washington, D.C., January 30, 2003

POLITICAL ACTOR

"Tommy [Thompson, the U.S. Secretary of Health and Human Services] is a good listener, and he's a pretty good actor, too."

—*Waco, Texas, August 13, 2002*

TOPSY-TURVY

"The person who runs FEMA is someone who must have the trust of the president. Because the person who runs FEMA is the first voice, often times, of someone whose life has been turned upside down hears from."

—*Austin, Texas, January 4, 2001*

THAT AL-QAIDA GUY

"President Musharraf, he's still tight with us on the war against terror, and that's what I appreciate. He's a—he understands that we've got to keep al-Qaida on the run, and that by keeping him on the run, it's more likely we will bring him to justice."

—Ruch, Oregon, August 22, 2002

BOMBERS AWAY

"These people don't have tanks. They don't have ships. They hide in caves. They send suiciders out."

—*Portsmouth, New Hampshire, November 1, 2002*

FORE!

"I call upon all nations to do everything
they can to stop these terrorist killers.
Thank you. Now watch this drive."

—*August 4, 2002*

PROCESS I

"Oftentimes, we live in a processed world—
you know, people focus on the process and
not results."

—Washington, D.C., May 29, 2003

PROCESS II

"Security is the essential roadblock to
achieving the road map to peace."

—Washington, D.C., July 25, 2003

NEIGHBORS

"The true strength of America happens when a neighbor loves a neighbor just like they'd like to be loved themselves."

—*Elizabeth, New Jersey, June 16, 2003*

GENEROSITY

"Our country puts $1 billion a year up to help feed the hungry. And we're by far the most generous nation in the world when it comes to that, and I'm proud to report that. This isn't a contest of who's the most generous. I'm just telling you as an aside. We're generous. We shouldn't be bragging about it. But we are. We're very generous."

—*Washington, D.C., July 16, 2003*

PROGRESS

"We are making steadfast progress."

—*Washington, D.C., June 9, 2003*

GULF SHRIMP

"I've got very good relations with President Mubarak and Crown Prince Abdullah and the King of Jordan, Gulf Coast countries."

—Washington, D.C., May 29, 2003

ICEBREAKER

"Thirdly, the explorationists are willing to only move equipment during the winter, which means they'll be on ice roads, and remove the equipment as the ice begins to melt, so that the fragile tundra is protected."

—*Conestoga, Pennsylvania May 18, 2001*

ENERGY POLICY

"We need an energy bill that encourages consumption."

—*Trenton, New Jersey, September 23, 2002*

DO OR DIE

"I haven't had a chance to talk, but I'm confident we'll get a bill that I can live with if we don't."

—Referring to the McCain-Kennedy patients' bill of rights, Brussels, Belgium, June 13, 2001

UPDATE

"We had a good cabinet meeting, talked about a lot of issues. Secretary of state and defense brought us up to date about our desires to spread freedom and peace around the world."

—Washington, D.C., August 1, 2003

SADDAM I

"The war on terror involves Saddam
Hussein because of the nature of Saddam
Hussein, the history of Saddam Hussein, and
his willingness to terrorize himself."

—*Grand Rapids, Michigan, January 29, 2003*

SADDAM II

"We ended the rule of one of history's worst tyrants, and in so doing, we not only freed the American people, we made our own people more secure."

—Crawford, Texas, May 3, 2003

SADDAM III

"There's no doubt in my mind that we should allow the world's worst leaders to hold America hostage, to threaten our peace, to threaten our friends and allies with the world's worst weapons."

—South Bend, Indiana, September 5, 2002

SADDAM IV

"I was proud the other day when both Republicans and Democrats stood with me in the Rose Garden to announce their support for a clear statement of purpose: you disarm, or we will."

—*Manchester, New Hampshire, October 5, 2002*

SHOWING SOME LEG

"Perhaps one way will be, if we use military force, in the post-Saddam Iraq the U.N. will definitely need to have a role. And that way it can begin to get its legs, legs of responsibility back."

—*the Azores, March 16, 2003*

WMD

"We've got hundreds of sites to exploit,
looking for the chemical and biological
weapons that we know Saddam Hussein had
prior to our entrance into Iraq."

—*Santa Clara, California, May 2, 2003*

WMP

"The law I sign today directs new funds and
new focus to the task of collecting vital
intelligence on terrorist threats and on
weapons of mass production."

—*Washington, D.C., November 27, 2002*

TOP ADVISER

"I don't bring God into my life to—to, you
know, kind of be a political person."

—*Interview with Tom Brokaw aboard Air Force One,*
April 24, 2003

GOD AS MY WITNESS

"I want to thank you for coming to the
White House to give me an opportunity to
urge you to work with these five senators
and three congressmen, to work hard to get
this trade promotion authority moving. The
power that be, well most of the power that
be, sits right here."

—*Washington, D.C., June 18, 2001*

CHAOS THEORY

"You know, it'll take time to restore chaos and order—order out of chaos. But we will."

—*Washington, D.C., April 13, 2003*

RETIRING

"Now, we talked to Joan Hanover. She and her husband, George, were visiting with us. They are near retirement—retiring—in the process of retiring, meaning they're very smart, active, capable people who are retirement age and are retiring."

—*Alexandria, Virginia, February 12, 2003.*

PUNDITS

"Many of the punditry—of course, not you [laughter]—but other punditry were quick to say, no one is going to follow the United States of America."

—*Washington, D.C., January 21, 2003*

31

GOING UNDERGROUND

"There's no cave deep enough for America, or dark enough to hide."

—Oklahoma City, August 29, 2002

NOW AND THEN

"One year ago today, the time for excuse making has come to an end."

—Washington, D.C., January 8, 2003

JUST CALLED TO SAY

"People say, how can I help on this war against terror? How can I fight evil? You can do so by mentoring a child; by going into a shut-in's house and say I love you."

—Washington, D.C., September 19, 2002

LOVING STUFF

"See, we love—we love freedom. That's what they didn't understand. They hate things; we love things. They act out of hatred; we don't seek revenge, we seek justice out of love."

—Oklahoma City, August 29, 2002

BRANCH I

"You see, the Senate wants to take away some of the powers of the administrative branch."

—*Washington, D.C., September 19, 2002*

BRANCH II

"I'd rather have them sacrificing on behalf of our nation than, you know, endless hours of testimony on congressional hill."

—*Fort Meade, Maryland, June 4, 2002*

FAILED OPERATION

"The trial lawyers are very politically powerful. . . . But here in Texas we took them on and got some good medical— medical malpractice."

—*Waco, Texas, August 13, 2002*

READY

"My answer is bring them on."

—On Iraqi militants attacking U.S. forces,
Washington, D.C., July 3, 2003

PITY THE FOOL

**"There's an old saying in Tennessee—I know
it's in Texas, probably in Tennessee—that
says, fool me once, shame on—shame on
you. Fool me—you can't get fooled again."**

—Nashville, Tennessee, September 17, 2002

NO BETTER

"The federal government and the state government must not fear programs who change lives, but must welcome those faith-based programs for the embetterment of mankind."

—*Stockton, California, August 23, 2002*

OUCH

"Let me tell you my thoughts about tax relief. When your economy is kind of ooching along, it's important to let people have more of their own money."

—*Boston, Massachusetts, October 4, 2002*

NOT SHARP

"Sometimes, Washington is one of these towns where the person—people who think they've got the sharp elbow is the most effective person."

—*New Orleans, Louisiana, December 3, 2002*

UNCONVINCING

"Nothing he [Saddam Hussein] has done has convinced me—I'm confident the secretary of defense—that he is the kind of fellow that is willing to forgo weapons of mass destruction, is willing to be a peaceful neighbor, that is—will honor the people— the Iraqi people of all stripes, will—values human life. He hasn't convinced me, nor has he convinced my administration."

—Crawford, Texas, August 21, 2002

FREEDOM

"In other words, I don't think people ought to be compelled to make the decision which they think is best for their family."

—*Washington, D.C., December 11, 2002*

43

COMPASSION

"The goals for this country are peace in the world. And the goals for this country are a compassionate American for every single citizen. That compassion is found in the hearts and souls of the American citizens."

—Washington, D.C., December 19, 2002

SHIFTY

"You've also got to measure in order to begin to effect change that's just more— when there's more than talk, there's just actual—a paradigm shift."

—Washington, D.C., July 1, 2003

BULLY FOR US I

"I don't want nations feeling like that they can bully ourselves and our allies. . . ."

BULLY FOR US II

". . . at the same time I want to reduce our own nuclear capacities to the level commiserate with keeping the peace."

—*Des Moines, Iowa, October 23, 2000*

HOME SWEET HOME

"There's no bigger task than protecting the homeland of our country."

—*Stockton, California, August 23, 2002*

IMMIGRATION

"It's very interesting when you think about it, the slaves who left here to go to America, because of their steadfast and their religion and their belief in freedom, helped change America."

—*Dakar, Senegal, July 8, 2003 (Thanks to Michael Shively)*

STAYING PUT

"I love the idea of a school in which people come to get educated and stay in the state in which they're educated."

—*Waco, Texas, August 13, 2002*

JUST SAY NO

"I urge the leaders in Europe and around the world to take swift, decisive action against terror groups such as Hamas, to cut off their funding, and to support—cut funding and support, as the United States has done."

—*Washington, D.C., June 25, 2003*

WORLD GOV I

"I need to be able to move the right people to the right place at the right time to protect you, and I'm not going to accept a lousy bill out of the United Nations Senate."

—South Bend, Indiana, October 31, 2002

WORLD GOV II

"John Thune has got a common-sense
vision for good forest policy. I look forward
to working with him in the United Nations
Senate to preserve these national
heritages."

—*South Bend, Indiana, October 31, 2002*

UNCONSTITUTIONAL

"Any time we've got any kind of inkling that somebody is thinking about doing something to an American and something to our homeland, you've just got to know we're moving on it, to protect the United Nations Constitution, and at the same time, we're protecting you."

—Aberdeen, South Dakota, October 31, 2002

GONE UNDER

"I'm plowed of the leadership of Chuck Grassley and Greg Ganske and Jim Leach."

—Davenport, Iowa, September 16, 2002

HUGGER

"There's only one person who hugs the
mothers and the widows, the wives and
the kids upon the death of their loved one.
Others hug but having committed
the troops, I've got an additional
responsibility to hug and that's me
and I know what it's like."

—*Washington, D.C., December 11, 2002*

DEATH AND TAXES

"I firmly believe the death tax is good for
people from all walks of life all throughout
our society."

—*Waco, Texas, August 13, 2002*

BEWITCHED

"We've had a great weekend here in the Land of the Enchanted."

—Albuquerque, New Mexico, May 12, 2003 (New Mexico's state nickname is "Land of Enchantment")

WHERE IT LIES

"I think we're making progress. We understand where the power of this country lay. It lays in the hearts and souls of Americans. It must lay in our pocketbooks. It lays in the willingness for people to work hard. But as importantly, it lays in the fact that we've got citizens from all walks of life, all political parties, that are willing to say, I want to love my neighbor. I want to make somebody's life just a little bit better."

—*Concord, North Carolina, April 11, 2001*

SPEECH

"I suspect that had my dad not been president, he'd be asking the same questions: How'd your meeting go with so-and-so? . . . How did you feel when you stood up in front of the people for the State of the Union Address—state of the budget address, whatever you call it."

—*Interview with* The Washington Post, *March 9, 2001*

WHERE HE'S GOING

"I think there is some methodology in my travels."

—Washington, D.C., March 5, 2001

SELF-HELP

"Whatever it took to help Taiwan defend theirself."

—On how far we'd be willing to go to defend Taiwan, Good Morning America, April 25, 2001

HON

"You might want to comment on that, Honorable."

—To New Jersey's secretary of state, the Honorable DeForest Soaries, Jr., as quoted in The Washington Post, *July 15, 2000*

WINGS

"We've got pockets of persistent poverty in our society, which I refuse to declare defeat—I mean, I refuse to allow them to continue on. And so one of the things that we're trying to do is to encourage a faith-based initiative to spread its wings all across America, to be able to capture this great compassionate spirit."

—*O'Fallon, Missouri, March 18, 2002*

FUZZY MATH

"We've tripled the amount of money—
I believe it's from $50 million up to $195
million available."

—*Lima, Peru, March 23, 2002*

READING

"One reason I like to highlight reading is, reading is the beginnings of the ability to be a good student. And if you can't read, it's going to be hard to realize dreams; it's going to be hard to go to college. So when your teachers say, read—you ought to listen to her."

—*Washington, D.C., February 9, 2001*

TROOPER

"I do think we need for a troop to be able to house his family. That's an important part of building morale in the military."

—*Tyndall Air Force Base, Florida, March 12, 2001*

COUNTDOWN

BUSH: First of all, *Cinco de Mayo* is not the independence day. That's *dieciséis de Septiembre,* and—
MATTHEWS: What's that in English?
BUSH: Fifteenth of September. [*Dieciséis de Septiembre* is September 16]

—Hardball, *MSNBC, May 31, 2000*

INSECURITIES

"We're working with Chancellor Schröder
on what's called 10 plus 10 over 10: $10
billion from the U.S., $10 billion from other
members of the G7 over a 10-year period, to
help Russia securitize the dismantling—the
dismantled nuclear warheads."

—Berlin, Germany, May 23, 2002

CANCEL MINE

"You subscribe politics to it. I subscribe freedom to it."

—Responding to a question about whether he and Al Gore were making the Elián Gonzalez case a political issue, Palm Beach, Florida, April 6, 2000

THINKING

"Then I went for a run with the other dog
and just walked. And I started thinking
about a lot of things. I was able to—I can't
remember what it was. Oh, the inaugural
speech, started thinking through that."

—U.S. News & World Report, *January 22, 2001*

ENEMIES

"But the true threats to stability and peace
are these nations that are not very
transparent, that hide behind the—that
don't let people in to take a look and see
what they're up to. They're very kind of
authoritarian regimes. The true threat is
whether or not one of these people decide,
peak of anger, try to hold us hostage,
ourselves; the Israelis, for example, to
whom we'll defend, offer our defenses; the
South Koreans."

—*Washington, D.C., March 13, 2001*

CAN'T DO

"Can't living with the bill means it won't become law."

—Referring to the McCain-Kennedy patients' bill of rights, Brussels, Belgium, June 13, 2001

UNDECIDED

"We don't believe in planners and deciders
making the decisions on behalf of
Americans."

—Scranton, Pennsylvania, September 6, 2000

CERTAINLY

"This is a world that is much more uncertain
than the past. In the past we were certain,
we were certain it was us versus the
Russians in the past. We were certain, and
therefore we had huge nuclear arsenals
aimed at each other to keep the peace.
That's what we were certain of. . . . You see,
even though it's an uncertain world, we're
certain of some things. We're certain that

even though the 'evil empire' may have passed, evil still remains. We're certain there are people that can't stand what America stands for. . . . We're certain there are madmen in this world, and there's terror, and there's missiles and I'm certain of this, too: I'm certain to maintain the peace, we better have a military of high morale, and I'm certain that under this administration, morale in the military is dangerously low."

—*Albuquerque, New Mexico, May 31, 2000*

TO COIN A PHRASE

"Now, there are some who would like to rewrite history—revisionist historians is what I like to call them."

—Elizabeth, New Jersey, June 16, 2003.

KARMA

"You cannot lead America to a positive tomorrow with revenge on one's mind. Revenge is so incredibly negative."

—*Interview with* The Washington Post, *March 23, 2000*

PHILOSOPHY

"It's important for young men and women who look at the Nebraska champs to understand that quality of life is more than just blocking shots."

—*To the University of Nebraska women's volleyball team, the 2001 national champions, Washington, D.C., May 31, 2001*

SOCIAL ANIMAL

"The students at Yale came from all different backgrounds and all parts of the country. Within months, I knew many of them."

—*From* A Charge to Keep, *by George W. Bush, published November 1999*

ME

"I'm also not very analytical. You know I
don't spend a lot of time thinking about
myself, about why I do things."

—*Aboard Air Force One, June 4, 2003*

TO BE OR NOT

"Anyway, after we go out and work our
hearts out, after you go out and help us turn
out the vote, after we've convinced the
good Americans to vote, and while they're
at it, pull that old George W. lever, if I'm the
one, when I put my hand on the Bible, when
I put my hand on the Bible, that day when
they swear us in, when I put my hand on the
Bible, I will swear to not—to uphold the
laws of the land."

—*Toledo, Ohio, October 27, 2000*

Photo Credits

AFP/CORBIS: 12, 16, 20, 23, 43, 52, 53, 79, 80

AP/Wide World Photos: 2, 30, 35

William Thomas Cain/Getty Images: 44

Larry Downing/Reuters/Landov: 8, 32, 33, 69, 73

Brooks Kraft/CORBIS: 28, 63

Kevin Lamarque/Reuters/Landov: 5, 18, 22, 37, 57, 58, 61, 71

Win McNamee/Reuters/Landov: 67, 75

Jeff Mitchell/Reuters/Landov: 6, 59

John Mottern/Getty Images: 47

William Philpott/Reuters/Landov: 41, 82

Reuters NewMedia Inc./CORBIS: 11, 15, 24, 48, 51, 55

Brendan Smialowski/Getty Images: 64

Mark Wilson/Getty Images: 38

Alex Wong/Getty Images: 76